40 Royal Wedding Recipes

Celebrate Prince Harry and Meghan Markle's Big Day by Appointment Only!

By

Martha Stephenson

Copyright 2018 Martha Stephenson

License Notes

No part of this Book can be reproduced in any form or by any means including print, electronic, scanning or photocopying unless prior permission is granted by the author.

All ideas, suggestions and guidelines mentioned here are written for informative purposes. While the author has taken every possible step to ensure accuracy, all readers are advised to follow information at their own risk. The author cannot be held responsible for personal and/or commercial damages in case of misinterpreting and misunderstanding any part of this Book

Table of Contents

Introduction 6

Canapés and Appetizers 8

    Asparagus with Hollandaise Sauce 9

    Beetroot Blinis with Smoked Salmon 12

    California Sushi Canapés 14

    Cornish Crab Soup with Sherry 18

    Coronation Chicken Curry Salad 20

    Eggs Drumkilbo 24

    English Cucumber Tea Sandwiches with Lemon-Dill Spread 28

    Haddock Fishcakes with Pea Guacamole 30

    Italian-Style Wedding Soup 34

    Lime Fish Tacos 36

    Walnut-Crusted Baked Goat Cheese 38

    Welsh Rarebit Bites 41

Windsor Consommé 43

Mains 45

Cretan Wedding Risotto 46

Fish Quenelles with Lobster Sauce 49

Goat Curry 52

Koenigsberger Wedding Noodles 55

Partridge Casserole 58

Prince William's Lamb Burger 61

Roast Chicken with Radishes by Royal Engagement 63

Russian Beef Stroganoff 66

Saddle of Lamb with Roasted Vegetables 69

Salmon en Croûte with Spinach and Wild Rice Pilaf 72

Salmon Supreme a La Reine Mary with Duchesse Potatoes .. 75

Smoked Haddock Pie in Puff Pastry 78

Turkey Meatballs 81

Sweets 84

Bombe Glacee 85

4

Caramel Banana Cake Bars 87

Chocolate Fridge Cake 90

Danish Wedding Cookies 92

Eton Mess Raspberry Royale 94

Jelly-Filled Heart Donuts 96

Lavender Shortbread 99

Lemon and Elderflower Drizzle Cake 101

Mexican Wedding Biscuits 104

Peppermint Ice Cream 106

Princess Diana's Boozy Bread and Butter Pudding 109

Queen of Puddings 112

Rhubarb Creme Brulee 115

Spanish Wedding Cake 117

About the Author 119

Author's Afterthoughts 121

Introduction

In 2018 with the wedding between American actress, Meghan Markle and HRH Prince Harry, Royal wedding fever swept the world.

Here are some fun facts about past British Royal weddings:

- The first Royal wedding took place in Westminster Abbey over 900 years ago when Henry I married Princess Matilda of Scotland
- Queen Victoria chose to wear a white dress when she said yes to Prince Albert. She was, in fact, responsible for launching the tradition of walking down the aisle in white

- When Princess Elizabeth married Philip, her dashing Greek fiancé, she paid for the fabric for her wedding dress using ration coupons
- Queen Elizabeth's younger sister, Princess Margaret, married Antony Armstrong-Jones in 1960 with the wedding broadcast by the BBC seen by 300 million people worldwide
- Princess Anne and Captain Mark Phillip's wedding cake stood 5ft 6ins tall. Incidentally, the same height as the Princess!
- Diana's wedding train, at 25ft long, is the longest train in royal history
- The marriage of Prince William and Kate Middleton cost British taxpayers 34 million pounds
- At 37 years of age, Meghan Markle is the most mature royal bride

A Royal wedding is always a cause for celebration, but you don't have to be noble to enjoy your big day.

We have brought together 40 Royal Wedding Recipes to help you celebrate your own special occasion or wedding party!

Canapés and Appetizers

Asparagus with Hollandaise Sauce

Follow in the footsteps of one of the world's most famous couples. No, not Kim and Kanye but William and Kate, enjoy these delicious canapés which formed part of their wedding luncheon.

Servings: 4

Total Time: 25mins

Ingredients:

- 1 pound asparagus
- Hollandaise sauce:
- 10 tbsp unsalted butter
- 3 egg yolks
- 1 tbsp freshly squeezed lemon juice
- ½ tsp salt
- Pinch of cayenne

Directions:

1. First, prepare the asparagus by breaking off the tough ends; you can do this with your fingers. Carefully, bend each spear near the end until it naturally breaks.

2. Take a veggie peeler and peel off a very fine layer of the outer skin of the lower 2-3" of the spears.

3. Add ½" of cold water to a shallow pan with steamer rack.

4. To prepare the sauce, in a small pan, melt the butter.

5. Add the egg yolks, freshly squeezed lemon juice, salt and cayenne to a food blender and at moderately-high speed, blend until light in color.

6. Reduce the blender speed to its very lowest setting and slowly drizzle in the melted, hot butter while the motor is still running. Continue blending for 2-3 seconds until all of the butter is combined.

7. Taste and season with either salt or fresh lemon juice as necessary. Put to one side and keep warm while you steam the asparagus.

8. To steam the asparagus, bring the water in the shallow pan to boil.

9. Arrange the asparagus in a single layer on the rack and cover with a lid.

10. Steam for between 3-5 minutes, until just al dente. Timings very much depend on the thickness of the spears.

11. To serve, arrange the asparagus on a white china plate and cover with Hollandaise sauce.

Beetroot Blinis with Smoked Salmon

Prince William and Kate Middleton's wedding in 2011 was a really grand affair, and the Queen hosted a reception for a colossal 650 guests, offering a huge selection of canapés. In fact, around 10,000 canapes were on the menu, and beetroot blinis with smoked salmon was just one of them.

Servings: 40

Total Time: 30mins

Ingredients:

- 1 medium cooked beetroot
- 6 ounces Greek yogurt
- 2 medium eggs
- ½ tsp bicarb of soda
- 5 ounces self-raising flour
- Cream cheese (to serve)
- Salt and pepper
- Smoked salmon trimmings (to serve)
- Dill sprigs (to serve)

Directions:

1. First, make the blini batter. Using a stick blender, blend the beetroot along with the yogurt until silky smooth. Whisk in the eggs, followed by the bicarb of soda and flour.

2. Using a teaspoon, drop the mixture into a hot frying pan. Turn the mixture over as soon as small bubbles begin to form on the surface of each one, then cook for 30 seconds. Transfer to a wire baking rack.

3. Repeat the process until all of the batter is used.

4. Smear cream cheese onto each blini and season.

5. Top with salmon trimmings and garnish with dill.

California Sushi Canapés

We are sure that hailing from California, Meghan Markle would give these sushi canapés the royal seal of approval.

Servings: 32

Total Time: 1hour 45mins

Ingredients:

Rice:

- 1 cup water
- ¾ cup uncooked sushi rice
- 2 tbsp seasoned rice vinegar

Sauce:

- 3 tbsp mayonnaise
- 2 tsp ginger root (finely chopped)
- 1 tsp roasted red chili paste

Canapes:

- 1 small English cucumber
- 1 (8x7") nori sheet (cut into 8 rows by 4 rows)
- 2 tbsp sesame seed (toasted)
- ½ avocado (peeled, pitted, cut into small pieces)
- ½ red bell pepper (finely chopped)

Directions:

1. In a pan, heat 1 cup of water along with the sushi rice until boiling. Turn the heat down to low, cover with a lid and simmer for between 15-20 minutes, or until tender.

2. Transfer the rice to a mixing bowl, tossing with two forks to speed up the cooling process.

3. A little at a time, add the vinegar, continually tossing.

4. Cover the bowl with a clean damp tea towel and allow the rice to cool to room temperature. This will take around 45 minutes.

5. In the meantime, in a bowl, combine the sauce ingredients; mayonnaise, ginger root and chili paste. Mix to combine, cover and transfer to the fridge until you are ready.

6. To assemble the canapés first cut the cucumber into 32 (1/4 ") thick slices and arrange them on a platter.

7. For each canapé, place 1 piece of nori on each slice of cucumber.

8. Top each one with ¼ tsp of sauce.

9. Using a teaspoon, scoop the rice, pressing it against the side of the bowl to ensure it holds the spoon shape and is packed.

10. Gently take the rice out of the spoon. Carefully dip the flat side into the sesame seeds and put, flat side facing downwards onto the sauce.

11. Top each with a small piece of avocado and pepper. Serve straight away.

12. Alternatively, cover and transfer to the fridge for no more than 2 hours.

Cornish Crab Soup with Sherry

The Duchess of Cornwall would certainly approve of this crab soup served with a swirl of double cream.

Servings: 8

Total Time: 40mins

Ingredients:

- 8 ounces fresh crab meat
- 3½ tbsp salted butter
- ½ cup plain flour
- 4 cups full-cream milk
- 5 cups chicken stock
- ¼ tsp grated nutmeg (grated)
- Salt and white pepper
- Pinch of saffron
- 2 tbsp dry sherry
- ½ cup heavy cream

Directions:

1. Separate the dark and white crab meat.

2. In a pan, melt the butter. Add the flour and while stirring, cook for a few minutes.

3. A little at a time, while stirring, pour in the milk along with the chicken stock.

4. Add the dark crab meat to the pan followed by the nutmeg, seasoning to taste.

5. Gently simmer for 12-15 minutes.

6. Sprinkle in a pinch of saffron and stir to combine.

7. Add the white crab meat along with the sherry and simmer for 4-5 minutes. Do not allow the soup to boil.

8. Swirl with cream before serving.

Coronation Chicken Curry Salad

Created for the Coronation lunch of Queen Elizabeth in 1953, this curried chicken salad is the perfect retro, royal wedding dish.

Servings: 6 cups

Total Time: 3hours

Ingredients:

- 10 whole black peppercorns
- 2 celery ribs (roughly chopped)
- 1 yellow onion (peeled, roughly chopped)
- 1 (4 pound) whole chicken
- 1 (2″) piece ginger (peeled, 2″ thinly sliced)
- 1 leek (roughly chopped)
- 1 garlic bulb (halved crosswise)
- 1 star anise
- ½ lemon (thinly sliced)
- ½ orange (thinly sliced)
- Kosher salt
- Water

Curry sauce:

- 3 tbsp unsalted butter
- 1 yellow onion (peeled, diced)
- 1 (1″) piece ginger (peeled, minced)
- 2 garlic cloves (peeled, finely chopped)
- 1 tbsp curry powder
- ¼ cup flour
- ¼ cup heavy cream
- 2 tbsp currants
- 2 tbsp dried apricots (finely chopped)
- 1¼ cups mayonnaise
- ½ cup Greek yogurt
- ¼ cup mango chutney
- 1 tbsp freshly squeezed lemon juice

- Freshly ground black pepper
- ½ cup toasted almonds (slivered)

Directions:

1. In a pan, add the peppercorns, celery, roughly chopped onion, chicken, sliced ginger, leek, along with the garlic bulb, star anise, and lemon, orange, and salt. Add sufficient water to cover by approximately 1".

2. Over high heat, bring to boil, before reducing the heat to moderately low, and while partially covered, simmer for 60 minutes.

3. Remove the pan from the heat and allow to cool.

4. Take the chicken out of the pan and set to one side.

5. Through a fine mesh strainer, pour the stock into a clean pan over high heat and bring to boil, cooking for 90 minutes, until reduced to no more than 1 cup. Set aside to cool.

6. In the meantime, remove the meat from the chicken, tearing into thick strips. Discard the bones along with the skin and transfer the meat to the fridge.

7. Next, prepare the sauce. Over moderate heat, in a pan, heat the butter.

8. Add the onion, followed by the ginger and garlic and while stirring, cook for between 3-5 minutes, until softened. Whisk in the curry powder and flour, cook for 2 more minutes.

9. Pour in the reduced stock and while constantly stirring, bring to boil, cooking until thickened. This will take no more than 1-2 minutes.

10. Remove the pan from the heat and add the cream, while gently stirring.

11. Pour the sauce through a fine, mesh strainer into a large mixing bowl, discarding any solids.

12. Stir in the currants along with the apricots and set aside to cool.

13. Add the mayo, yogurt, chutney and freshly squeezed lemon juice. Season and whisk well to incorporate.

14. Add the strips of chicken to the sauce, tossing to combine.

15. Transfer to the fridge to chill.

16. Garnish with almonds and serve.

Eggs Drumkilbo

Served at the 1986 wedding of Prince Andrew and his bride Sarah Ferguson, eggs drumkilbo are rumored to be the late Queen Mother's favorite.

Servings: 6

Total Time: 1hour 5mins

Ingredients:

- 2 (1½ pound) lobsters (cooked, cooled)
- 8 hard-boiled eggs (shelled, divided)
- 4 cups water
- 6 vine-ripe tomatoes
- 2 cups mayonnaise
- ½ cup tomato ketchup
- 1 tsp Worcestershire sauce
- Salt and freshly ground pepper
- 1 packet unflavored gelatin
- 1 cup sherry
- 6 medium shrimps
- 6 sprigs of parsley (to garnish)
- Lemon wedges (to serve)
- Thinly sliced buttered, brown bread (to serve)

Directions:

1. First, prepare the lobsters by removing the meat from the lobster claws and tails and cut into bite-size pieces.

2. Dice 6 of the hard-boiled eggs to the same size as the pieces of lobster.

3. In a heavy pan, bring the water to a rolling boil.

4. Cut the green stems from each of the tomatoes and plunge them into the boiling water for no more than 30 seconds and immediately remove to iced water and allow to stand for 6-8 minutes.

5. Carefully peel the skins away from the tomatoes and using kitchen paper towel, dry the tomato flesh.

6. Slice the tomatoes into four quarters and remove the membranes and seeds.

7. Dice the flesh into the same diced sized pieces as the lobster and egg.

8. In a non-metallic bowl, whisk the mayonnaise with the ketchup and Worcestershire sauce until incorporated.

9. Add the pieces of lobster and egg and stir to combine.

10. Add the tomatoes and gently fold. Taste and season.

11. Spoon the mixture into a glass serving dish, smoothing over the top to even.

12. In a small pan, soften the gelatin together with the sherry.

13. Over low heat, stir until totally dissolved.

14. Spoon a fine layer of the sherry over the top of the mixture and transfer to the fridge until set.

15. With an egg slicer, from the remaining 2 hard boiled eggs, slice 6 circles.

16. Brush the tops of each of the slices of egg with a little of the warmed gelatin.

17. Slice each shrimp in half across their length, dip them into the gelatin-sherry and arrange prettily on a slice of egg.

18. Transfer to the fridge, until set.

19. When set, carefully arrange each egg-shrimp garnish and use to decorate the lobster salad.

20. Garnish with a sprig of parsley and serve with wedges of lemon and thinly sliced brown, buttered bread.

English Cucumber Tea Sandwiches with Lemon-Dill Spread

Probably one of the most popular canapés ever created; English cucumber sandwiches are as British as Buckingham Palace, red telephone boxes and black cabs!

Servings: 24 sandwich triangles

Total Time: 2hours 15mins

Ingredients:

- 8 ounces cream cheese (softened)
- ⅓ cup fresh dill
- 2 tsp fresh lemon juice
- 1 tsp lemon zest (finely chopped)
- ¼ tsp salt
- Pinch black pepper
- 1 large English cucumber (thinly sliced using a mandolin)
- 12 slices think white bread
- Dill (to garnish)

Directions:

1. Add the cream cheese to a bowl and with a spoon, stir until lump-free. Add the dill, followed by the lemon juice and zest, salt and pepper and stir until incorporated.

2. Transfer the cream cheese to the fridge to chill for 2 hours to allow the flavors to intensify.

3. Remove the spread from the fridge half an hour before you are ready to assemble. This will allow it to spread more easily.

4. Spread the bread with the lemon dill mixture. Arrange the slices of cucumber on one side of each slice of bread and top with a second slice to create 6 sandwiches.

5. Remove the crusts and cut into triangles.

6. Garnish with fresh dill and serve.

Haddock Fishcakes with Pea Guacamole

William and Kate's canapé reception in 2011 featured smoked haddock fishcakes with pea guacamole. Fresh and delicious.

Servings: 75 (2") patties

Total Time: 8hours 40mins

Ingredients:

Pea Guacamole:

- 1 cup frozen peas (partially thawed)
- 2 Hass avocados (peeled, pitted)
- 2 tbsp freshly squeezed lime juice
- ½ red onion (peeled, diced into ⅛" pieces)
- 1 tomato (seeded, diced into ¼" pieces)
- 3 tbsp fresh cilantro (chopped)
- 1 jalapeno (seeded, minced)
- 1 tsp fresh garlic (peeled, minced)
- ½ tsp salt
- ¼ tsp freshly ground black pepper

Patties:

- Salt
- 4 pounds smoked haddock fillet
- 4 pounds cod fillet
- 2 large onions
- 8 large eggs
- 2 tbsp salt
- 2 tbsp sugar
- 1 tsp white pepper
- 2 cups matzah meal
- Sunflower oil

Directions:

1. For the guacamole: In a food blender, process the peas until lump-free and smooth.

2. In a bowl, mash the avocado using a fork.

3. Add the lime juice followed by the onion, tomato, cilantro, jalapeno, garlic, salt, and pepper.

4. Add the pea mash and mix to combine.

5. If you don't intend to serve immediately, press a piece of kitchen wrap onto the surface of the guacamole. This will stop it from browning.

6. For the fishcakes, first, wash and salt the haddock and cod and set to one side to drain.

7. Chop the onion into 1" chunks and transfer to a food processor along with the eggs, salt, sugar, and pepper. Process to a puree.

8. Transfer the puree to a bowl and add the matzah meal, stirring to combine. Set to one side and allow to swell.

9. Cut the haddock and cod into 1" chunks and add to the processor.

10. Process for 5 seconds until the haddock and cod are finely chopped. Add the fish to the puree and using a fork, blend.

11. As soon as the fish is completely processed, combine everything together and using your hands, mix.

12. Using clean hands form the mixture into evenly sized patties. If the mixture is too soft, stir in between 1-2 tbsp of matzah. Alternatively, if the mixture is a little thick, rinse out the process with 1-2 tbsp of water and stir. The patties should be approximately ¾" thick and 2" in diameter.

13. Set the mixture aside overnight in your fridge.

14. In a pan, fry sufficient oil to sufficiently cover the patties and deep fry.

15. Serve alongside the guacamole.

Italian-Style Wedding Soup

You are unlikely to see this super-quick wedding soup on the menu for Harry and Meghan's big day, but for us lesser mortals, this Italian dish is a must-try.

Servings: 2-4

Total Time: 20mins

Ingredients:

- 1 cup water
- 2 (14½ ounce) cans chicken broth
- 1 cup shell-shaped pasta
- 16 frozen meatballs (cooked)
- 2 cups fresh spinach (shredded)
- 1 cup store-bought pizza sauce

Directions:

1. In a pan, bring the water and the broth to a boil.

2. Add the pasta along with the meatballs and bring back to a boil. Cook for between 7-9 minutes, until the pasta, is al dente. Do not drain.

3. Turn the heat down, fold in the spinach leaves along with the pizza sauce and cook for between 1-2 minutes until heated through.

Lime Fish Tacos

Add a zippy, citrus twist to fish tacos with freshly squeezed lime juice and enjoy Meghan Markle's California favorite, Baja-style food.

Servings: 7

Total Time:

Ingredients:

- 1 clove garlic (peeled, minced)
- 2 tbsp butter
- 7 tsp freshly squeezed lime juice (divided)
- 1 pound skinless, red snapper fillets (cut into 1" cubes)
- ¼ tsp white pepper
- 2 tbsp low-fat sour cream
- 2 tbsp fat-free mayonnaise
- Dash hot pepper sauce
- 8 (8") tortillas (warmed)
- 1 cup shredded lettuce
- 1 cup chopped tomatoes

Directions:

1. In a skillet, fry the garlic in butter along with 5 tsp of freshly squeezed lime juice for 30 seconds.

2. Add the cubes of fish along with the white pepper. Over moderate heat, cook for 6-8 minutes or until the fish flakes easily when using a fork, gently and occasionally stirring.

3. In the meantime, combine the sour cream with the mayo, hot pepper sauce, and remaining freshly squeezed lime juice.

4. Add a spoonful of fish onto each of the tortillas.

5. Top with shredded lettuce, chopped tomatoes and a dollop of spicy sour cream.

6. Enjoy.

Walnut-Crusted Baked Goat Cheese

Palace kitchens are only capable of handling formal dinners for approximately 150 persons, and so this is probably why finger foods were served at William and Kate's reception. Roulade of Goats Cheese with Caramelized Walnuts was just one of the many dishes on offer.

Servings: 4

Total Time: 50mins

Ingredients:

- 2 (4 ounce) logs fresh goat cheese
- 1 cup whole California walnuts
- 2 tbsp fresh chives (roughly chopped)
- ¾ cup fresh mushrooms (quartered)
- 1 medium egg (beaten)
- 1 tbsp water
- Apple slices (to serve)
- French bread (to serve)

Directions:

1. Transfer the goat cheese to the freezer for 20 minutes. Using parchment paper, line a baking tray.

2. In a large, dry frying pan over moderately high heat, heat the walnuts, lightly toasting for 1-2 minutes.

3. Coarsely chop the toasted walnuts and add them along with the chives and mushrooms to a food processor, pulsing several times until incorporated. Transfer the mixture to a serving plate.

4. In a shallow bowl, beat the egg and whisk in 1 tbsp of water.

5. Dredge each piece of cheese in the egg and then roll in the walnut mixture, gently pressing the nuts into the cheese.

6. Place the walnut-crust goat cheese on the prepared baking tray.

7. When all of the cheese is coated, bake in the oven for between 10-12 minutes, or until warmed through. The cheese should be soft when pressed gently in the middle.

8. Serve the melted cheese with slices of apple or bread.

Welsh Rarebit Bites

In honor of William's late mother, the Princess of Wales, enjoy this traditional Welsh recipe.

Servings: 20

Total Time: 25mins

Ingredients:

- 2 tbsp unsalted butter
- 2 tbsp all-purpose flour
- 8 ounces aged Farmhouse cheddar (finely grated)
- ¾ cup stout beer
- 1 tbsp Worcestershire sauce
- 2 tsp dry mustard powder
- 1 tsp paprika
- 1 sweet baguette (cut into ¼ "slices, toasted)

Directions:

1. In a pan, combine the butter with the flour and cook over moderate heat until fragrant and toasted this will take around 3 minutes.

2. Add the cheese followed by the beer, Worcestershire sauce, mustard powder and paprika and cook, while constantly stirring, until the cheese is smooth and melted, 2-3 minutes.

3. Remove the pan from the heat.

4. Heat your broiler to high and place a rack in the lower third of the oven.

5. Using aluminum foil, line a baking sheet.

6. Arrange the slices of baguette on the sheet.

7. Spread 2 tsp of cheese mixture on one side of each slice.

8. Place the baking sheet under the broiler and toast until browned and bubbling, 1-2 minutes.

9. Serve at once.

Windsor Consommé

A favorite of the House of Windsor, this clear beef soup was served at the 1923 wedding of King George VI and Queen Elizabeth.

Servings: 4

Total Time: 45mins

Ingredients:

- 1 quart fresh beef stock
- Olive oil (to fry)
- 4 ounces button mushrooms (finely diced)
- 4 shallots (finely diced)
- 4 ounces Madeira
- Salt and pepper
- 1 (11 ounce) packet puff pastry
- Chopped parsley (to garnish)

Directions:

1. Strain the stock through a fine sieve.

2. In a pan, heat the oil and add the mushrooms along with the shallots and sauté for several minutes.

3. Pour in the Madeira and continue cooking for 30 seconds.

4. Add the beef stock along with the seasoning and bring to boil before simmering, uncovered for 20 minutes, or until reduced by 25%.

5. Divide the consommé between 4 bowls.

6. Cut the pastry into circles and add a pastry lid to each bowl.

7. Bake in the oven at 350 degrees F for between 8-10 minutes.

8. Garnish with parsley.

Mains

Cretan Wedding Risotto

In honor of HRH Prince Philip enjoy this traditional Greek wedding dish.

Servings: 6

Total Time: 40mins

Ingredients:

- 2 tbsp olive oil
- 1 tsp salt
- ½ tsp pepper
- 6 pieces of chicken, bone-in, skin-on
- 6 cups chicken stock (divided)
- 2 tbsp ghee
- 2 shallots (finely chopped)
- 1½ cups short-grain Arborio rice (rinsed, drained)
- 4 tbsp freshly squeezed lemon juice
- 1 tbsp lemon zest

Directions:

1. In an oven-proof pot or pan, heat the oil.

2. Combine the salt with the pepper and rub all over the chicken pieces.

3. Arrange the chicken in the pot, skin side facing downwards, and fry until crisp and golden. Flip the chicken over and continue frying.

4. Add 1½ cups of stock, cover with a lid and continue cooking.

5. In the meantime, in a skillet, heat the ghee. Add the shallots, frying until translucent.

6. Add the rice, stirring to toast and coat evenly in the ghee.

7. Gradually, pour in the remaining stock, stirring while it absorbs into the rice.

8. As soon as the stock is totally absorbed, add the freshly squeezed lemon juice and zest, stirring to incorporate.

9. Remove from the heat.

10. Ladle the rice onto a plate and top with the cooked chicken.

11. Serve.

Fish Quenelles with Lobster Sauce

Served at the wedding of Charles and Diana, this rich and decadent recipe is a perfect wedding dish.

Servings: 2-4

Total Time: 45mins

Ingredients:

Quenelles (Dumplings):

- ¾ pound haddock fillets (cut into cubes)
- ¾ cup 35% cream
- 1 medium egg
- Pinch of ground nutmeg
- Salt and pepper
- Fresh chervil sprigs (to garnish)

Lobster Sauce:

- 1 shallot (chopped)
- 1 cup crushed lobster carcass
- 1 tbsp olive oil
- 2 tbsp dry white wine
- 2 tbsp butter
- 2 tbsp flour
- 1¼ cups whole milk
- Salt and white pepper

Directions:

1. First prepare the dumplings by processing the haddock to a puree.

2. Pour in the cream, egg, and add the nutmeg, and process until silky smooth, scrape the bowl as needed and season.

3. Using 2 tablespoons, shape the dumplings with approximately 3 tbsp of the fish mixture for each and carefully drop them in a pan of simmering, salted water. Cook in batches of 6 for between 3-4 minutes. Drain and keep the dumplings warm.

4. For the sauce, in a pan brown the shallots along with the lobster carcass in the olive oil. Deglaze the pan with the white wine. Add the butter and sprinkle in the flour. Cook for 60 minutes, while constantly stirring.

5. Pour in the milk and bring to boil, constantly stirring. Gently simmer for a few minutes, before straining and seasoning.

6. Evenly divide the lobster sauce between 4 shallow dishes and top with the quenelles.

7. Garnish with fresh chervil.

8. Alternatively, arrange the quenelles in a serving dish, pour the lobster sauce over the top and brown under the broiler.

Goat Curry

Apparently, Prince Harry loves a hot and spicy goat curry which he first tasted during his time spent in Afghanistan. He isn't the only member of the Royal Family with a taste for curry though; his father Prince Philip also enjoys a Ruby Murray (cockney slang for curry).

Servings: 4-6

Total Time: 5hours 40mins

Ingredients:

- 2 pounds goat meat
- 2 red onions (peeled, chopped)
- 1½" knob fresh ginger (minced)
- 3 garlic cloves (peeled, minced)
- 4 whole cloves (ground)
- 1 bay leaf
- 1 tbsp ghee
- 2 cardamom pods (ground)
- 1 tbsp coriander powder
- 1 tsp cumin powder
- 2 tsp salt
- 1 tsp turmeric powder
- 1 tsp Kashmiri chili powder
- 1 tsp paprika
- 1-2 Serrano peppers (minced)
- 1 (28 ounce) can diced tomatoes
- 1 tsp garam masala
- ½ -1 cup water

Directions:

1. In a crock pot, add the goat meat, red onions, ginger, garlic, cloves, bay leaf, ghee, ground cardamom, coriander, cumin, salt, turmeric powder, chili powder, paprika, and minced pepper.

2. Cook on high heat for 4 hours, stirring every 60 minutes.

3. After the 4 hours have elapsed, add the diced tomatoes, followed by the garma massala and water. The amount of water will depend on how thick you like your curry.

4. Continue to cook on high for an additional 60 minutes, until the meat is fork tender.

Koenigsberger Wedding Noodles

Just over a century ago, King George V changed the British royal family's name from the German Saxe-Coburg to the very English, Windsor. These German-style wedding noodles pay homage to the family's true Germanic roots.

Servings: 4

Total Time: 45mins

Ingredients:

- 2 tsp butter
- 1 small onion (peeled, cut into small cubes)
- ¾ cup whipping cream
- ½ cup whole milk
- 6-½ oz broad egg noodles (Hochzeitsnudeln)
- ¾ cup German bratwurst sausage (raw, casings removed)
- 2 tsp capers
- ½ cup chives (washed, dried, diced)
- Pinch of salt
- Dash of pepper
- Dash freshly ground nutmeg
- Sprinkle of fresh lemon juice
- ½ tsp cornflour

Directions:

1. In a pan, melt the butter. Add the onions and cook until softened.

2. Pour in the whipping cream and whole milk and on low heat cook the sauce for 4-5 minutes.

3. Cook the noodles in a pan of salted water, according to the package instructions.

4. Using clean, damp hands form the sausage meat into small dumplings.

5. Add the dumplings along with the capers to the sauce, cover with a lid and simmer for several minutes until cooked through.

6. Drain the cooked noodles.

7. Season with a pinch of salt and a dash of pepper, followed by a dash of nutmeg, and a sprinkling of lemon juice. Stir in the cornflour if needed, to thicken.

8. Add the noodles to the dumpling-caper sauce and top with more chives.

Partridge Casserole

Princess Elizabeth and Philip Mountbatten were married in 1947 just after World War 2, which meant the big day was a modest affair. The couple dined on a fish appetizer followed by partridge casserole.

Servings: 6

Total Time: 1hour 40mins

Ingredients:

- 4-5 tbsp virgin olive oil
- 6 partridges (you may substitute for pheasant)
- 6 thick rashers streaky bacon (diced)
- 2 large onions (peeled, finely chopped)
- 4 garlic cloves (peeled, sliced)
- 3 medium carrots (sliced)
- 2 tsp black peppercorns
- 2 bay leaves
- Salt
- 4 sprigs of thyme
- 1 (750ml) bottle dry white wine
- 2 tbsp sherry vinegar
- 2 cups chicken stock
- Drop of cream or crème fraiche (optional)
- Mashed potatoes (optional)
- 5 sprigs flat-leaf parsley (chopped)

Directions:

1. Preheat the main oven to 360 degrees F.

2. Heat the oil in a large casserole dish.

3. Add the partridges to the dish and over moderate heat, brown on all sides. Remove from the dish.

4. Add the bacon along with the onion and fry until the bacon is opaque.

5. Add the garlic to the dish followed by the carrots and peppercorn, gently frying for several minutes until the onion is opaque.

6. Return the partridges to the casserole dish and add the bay leaves, followed by a pinch of salt, and the thyme. Pour in the wine, vinegar and chicken stock. Cover the dish with a lid and simmer in the oven for between 45-60 minutes.

7. Add a drop of cream at the last minute and stir to combine.

8. Remove to a serving dish.

9. Serve with mashed potatoes.

10. Serve on piping hot plates with a spoonful or two of the sauce and some creamy mashed potato. Garnish with parsley.

Prince William's Lamb Burger

We are sure that if Prince William had his way these delicious, meaty lamb burgers would be served on all royal occasions. In fact, when he served at RAF Valley, they were said to be his go-to meal.

Servings: 6

Total Time: 30mins

Ingredients:

- 1 pound lamb mince
- 1 large red onion (peeled, finely chopped)
- 2 tbsp ready-made mint sauce
- 1 clove garlic (peeled, finely chopped)
- 2 tbsp mixed herbs
- 3 tbsp paprika
- Salt
- Freshly ground black pepper
- 6 burger buns (split, toasted)
- 6 slices Mature Cheddar cheese
- 6 slices cooked cured bacon
- 6 medium eggs (fried)

Directions:

1. Preheat the main oven to 350 degrees F.

2. In a bowl combine the lamb mince, red onion, mint sauce, garlic, mixed herbs, paprika, salt, and pepper and using clean hands, mix until combined.

3. Form the mixture into 6 evenly-sized patties and transfer to the oven for 25-30 minutes, until sufficiently cooked through.

4. Serve in a toasted bun with a slice of Cheddar cheese, bacon and a fried egg.

Roast Chicken with Radishes by Royal Engagement

Prince Harry recently revealed to BBC News that he proposed to Meghan Markle over a home-cooked dinner of roast chicken. The young actress reveals that a good roast chicken recipe is a real game-changer.

Servings: 2-3

Total Time: 1hour 40mins

Ingredients:

- 1 (4-4 ½ pound) roasting chicken
- Kosher salt
- Freshly ground black pepper
- 1 fresh lemon (cut into quarters)
- 6 thyme sprigs
- ½ pound Heirloom radishes (trimmed, scrubbed)
- 3 tbsp unsalted butter (melted)

Directions:

1. Preheat the main oven to 425 degrees F.

2. Lay the chicken, breast side facing upwards in a baking dish, sufficiently large enough to hold the roasting chicken and radishes. Sprinkle salt and pepper inside the chicken's cavity along with the lemon and sprigs of thyme.

3. Using kitchen string, tie the legs together and tuck the wings under the body.

4. Cut any radishes that are on the large size into two and scatter around the bird.

5. Pat the chicken dry with kitchen paper towels and brush melted butter all over the chicken and radishes. Season liberally.

6. Roast in the preheated oven until the juices run clear when cut between the thigh and leg. This will take around 70-75 minutes.

7. Cover the baking pan with foil and put aside to rest at room temperature for 12-15 minutes.

8. Carve; serve with the radishes along with the pan juices.

Russian Beef Stroganoff

Breaking with royal tradition, Prince Edward and Sophie Rhys-Jones opted, in June 1999, to serve their guests with a buffet lunch. Their Russian style menu included Beef Stroganoff.

Servings: 4-6

Total Time: 55mins

Ingredients:

- 1½ pounds beef tenderloin (sliced into 2" long, thin strips)
- Salt and black pepper
- 2 onions (peeled, finely chopped)
- 4 ounces butter
- 4 ounces button mushrooms (sliced)
- 1 tbsp all-purpose flour
- ½ cup beef stock
- Pinch dry mustard
- 1 tbsp tomato paste
- ½ cup sour cream
- 6 ounces dry white wine

To serve:

- Pan-fried potatoes
- Pickles (sliced)
- Sour cream

Directions:

1. Season the beef with salt and black pepper.

2. In a large pan, sauté the onions together with the butter, until translucent.

3. Add the mushrooms to the pan and fry until collapsed, approximately 2 minutes.

4. Add the strips of beef and fry for 5 minutes before stirring in the flour.

5. In a bowl, combine the beef stock with the mustard and tomato paste and stir until totally blended. Pour the mixture into the pan and bring to boil, before lowering the heat and simmering on low for 15 minutes, or until the meat is cooked to your preference.

6. Temper the sour cream along with 2-3 ladles of hot cooking liquid. Pour in the wine.

7. Return the now tempered mixture to the pan and heat until sufficiently thickened.

8. Taste and season accordingly.

9. Serve with pan-fried potatoes, pickles and a jug of sour cream.

Saddle of Lamb with Roasted Vegetables

The Duke and Duchess of Cambridge were married in April, so it seems only fitting that they took advantage of the flavors of spring with organic lamb and fresh garden veggies.

Servings: 3

Total Time: 5hours 30mins

Ingredients:

Lamb:

- 1 pound saddle of lamb (bone-in)
- 1 tsp olive oil
- 3 garlic cloves (peeled, crushed)
- 1 tsp thyme
- 1 tsp rosemary
- Olive oil (to cook)
- Roasted vegetables:
- 4 large potatoes
- 1 large sweet potato
- ½ medium carrot
- ½ bunch of parsley
- ½ tsp thyme
- ½ tsp paprika
- ½ tsp coriander
- ½ tsp rosemary
- ½ tsp sea salt
- 2 tbsp olive oil

Sauce:

- 1 red onion (peeled, finely chopped)
- ¾ cup red dry wine
- 1 tsp honey
- Salt and pepper
- Pinch of thyme
- Pinch of rosemary

Directions:

1. First taking care not to damage the meat, wash and pat dry the lamb. Remove any excess fat and put to one side.

2. To prepare the marinade, rub the lamb with the olive oil, garlic, thyme, and rosemary and set to one side for 3-4 hours.

3. Preheat the main oven to 400 degrees F.

4. To prepare the roasted veggies; cut the potatoes and carrots into strips. Arrange the strips, in a single layer, on a baking tray. Chop the parsley and sprinkle it over the veggies along with the thyme, paprika, coriander, rosemary, and sea salt. Cover with olive oil and place in the oven.

5. Heat the olive oil in a skillet and gently brown the saddle of lamb for a couple of minutes each side. Transfer the lamb to an ovenproof casserole dish, bone side facing upwards and cover with kitchen foil. Reserve the juices in the pan.

6. Transfer the meat to the oven on a higher rack than the veggies and bake the meat and veggies for 20 minutes. Stir the veggies every 5 minutes or so.

7. Meanwhile, prepare the sauce. In the same pan, unwashed, that you used to brown the lamb in, fry the fat, set aside earlier, along with the finely chopped onions. Pour in the wine, add the honey followed by a pinch of salt, pepper, thyme, and rosemary and cook until reduced.

8. To assemble. Cut the lamb into chops, serve with the roasted vegetables and the wine sauce.

Salmon en Croûte with Spinach and Wild Rice Pilaf

The perfect wedding dish, salmon in pastry, served with a wild rice pilaf, which incidentally formed part of Prince Edward and Sophie Rhys-Jones buffet wedding lunch in 1999.

Servings: 2

Total Time: 1 hour

Ingredients:

- ⅓ bunch fresh spinach
- Fresh juice and zest of ½ a medium lemon
- 1 tbsp heavy cream
- Handful of parsley
- 1 sheet of frozen puff pastry (defrosted)
- 2 (6 ounce) salmon fillets
- Melted butter (to brush)
- Sea salt

Pilaf:

- ½ cup wild rice
- 1 cup jasmine rice
- 2 tbsp butter
- ¼ cup yellow onion (peeled, diced)
- ½ cup frozen peas
- Pinch of thyme

Directions:

1. In a sauté pan, wilt the spinach along with the fresh lemon juice and lemon zest. Remove the pan from the heat, add the cream and parsley and stir to combine.

2. Cut the thawed pastry into two halves.

3. Lay a salmon fillet on each pastry half and top with the spinach-parsley mixture.

4. Carefully fold the pastry over the salmon, gently pinching the edges to form a parcel. Lightly brush the pastry parcel with butter.

5. Place in an oven set at 400 degrees F and bake for half an hour.

6. In the meantime, and while the salmon cooks, prepare the rice pilaf.

7. Using a rice cooker, cook the rice, removing it from the heat as soon as it is cooked.

8. While the rice cools, in a pan, heat the butter.

9. Add the onions and cook until softened and translucent.

10. Add the peas, while stirring along with the thyme and over low heat cook for 7-8 minutes.

11. Finally, add the cooked rice, while stirring to ensure the rice is combined and coated.

12. Serve.

Salmon Supreme a La Reine Mary with Duchesse Potatoes

Recreate the dish enjoyed at the 1923 wedding of Prince Albert and Elizabeth Bowes-Lyon.

Servings: 4

Total Time: 1hour 30mins

Ingredients:

Sauce:

- Oil (to sauté)
- Butter (to sauté)
- ½ onion (peeled, finely diced)
- 1 stick celery (finely diced)
- ½ fennel bulb (finely diced)
- 4 ounces dry white wine
- ¾ pint double cream infused with 1 fresh bay leaf
- 4 sprigs dill (finely chopped)
- Salt and pepper
- 4 (6 ounce) salmon fillets

Potatoes:

- 2 pounds potatoes (peeled)
- 6 ounces butter
- 6 ounces double cream
- Salt and black pepper

Directions:

1. First, make the sauce. In a pan, heat the oil along with the butter. Add the onion along with the celery and fennel and fry for 3-4 minutes.

2. Pour in the wine and bring to boil, before simmering uncovered for 15-20 minutes, until reduced by around 50%.

3. Add the cream along with the bay leaf; bring to boil, before simmering for 10 minutes, to reduce by 25%.

4. Sieve the mixture to remove all the veggie bits. Adjust the seasonings and add the chopped dill.

5. In the meantime, season the salmon.

6. In a hot pan, seal the fish before roasting, uncovered in the oven at 350 degrees F, for 10 minutes.

7. To prepare the potatoes, in a pan of boiling, salted water, boil the potatoes until fork tender. Remove from the pan and mash. Add the butter, cream, and seasoning. Whisk until lump-free and smooth.

8. Pipe the creamy mash onto a baking sheet and brown in the oven along with the fish for 10 minutes.

Smoked Haddock Pie in Puff Pastry

This recipe is easy to make and very tasty. It is a variation of the pie served at the 1999 wedding of the Queen's youngest son, Prince Edward and Sophie Rhys-Jones.

Servings: 2

Total Time: 1hour

Ingredients:

- 2 ounces boneless, skinless smoked haddock (cut into bite-sized pieces)
- 1 tbsp crème fraiche
- Pinch of black pepper
- Handful of watercress (washed, dried)
- Flour
- 4½ ounces puff pastry
- Water

Directions:

1. Preheat the main oven to 425 degrees F.

2. Put the pieces of fish in a bowl and add the crème fraiche along with a pinch of pepper.

3. Tear the leaves off the watercress stalks and add to the bowl. Stir and put the mixing bowl to one side.

4. Lightly flour a clean worktop.

5. Roll the pastry out on the worktop into a rectangular shape of approximately the size of a sheet of A5 paper.

6. Position the pastry with the short edge closest to you and place the fish mixture on the bottom half of the pastry, leaving a ½" border around all the edges.

7. Brush the pastry with a drop of water.

8. Fold the top portion of the pastry down to form an envelope shape, to cover the mixture.

9. Using clean fingers fold and gently press the edges together.

10. Take a kitchen knife, trim the edges and make a small slit in the top of the pastry to allow the steam to escape.

11. Transfer to the oven and bake until golden, this will take between 20-30 minutes.

Turkey Meatballs

It's no secret that Meghan Markle loves turkey, whether it's meatloaf, burgers or shepherd's pie. This recipe for meatballs is bound to feature on the couple's weekly meal plan. Let's hope the chefs at Buckingham Palace are up to the challenge!

Servings: 2-4

Total Time: 45mins

Ingredients:

- 1 small onion
- 2 cloves garlic
- 6 fresh sage leaves
- 6 basil leaves
- 4 sprigs thyme
- 1 large rosemary sprig
- ¼ cup Italian parsley
- Handful of arugula
- 1 pound ground turkey breast
- 1 tsp sea salt
- ½ tsp black pepper
- 4 cups store-bought tomato sauce (of choice)
- 3 tbsp olive oil

Directions:

1. In a food processor bowl, combine the onion with the garlic, sage, basil, thyme, rosemary, parsley and arugula and on pulse, process until finely chopped.

2. Transfer the mixture to a bowl and add the ground turkey and season with the sea salt and black pepper.

3. Using clean hands mix to combine before molding into balls.

4. Over low to warm heat, heat the tomato sauce in a pan.

5. In a large pan, heat the olive oil and in batches cook the meatballs, for 3-4 minutes, until browned all over.

6. Add the cooked meatballs to the tomato sauce, gently stir and cook for half an hour until cooked through.

7. Serve with pasta or a green salad.

Sweets

Bombe Glacee

Princess Elizabeth and Philip Mountbatten enjoyed this dessert at their wedding reception in 1947. It is said to be the Queen's favorite sweet treat.

Servings: 4-6

Total Time: 4hours 30mins

Ingredients:

- 1 fruit sponge cake (of choice)
- ½ cup chocolate syrup
- ½ quart chocolate or vanilla ice-cream (softened)
- 5 ¼ ounces bitter-sweet chocolate (chopped into pieces)

Directions:

1. Line a pudding bowl with kitchen wrap, allowing sufficient overhang to wrap the pudding entirely.

2. Slice the ready-made fruitcake into thin slices and position it around the bowl's lining to cover the base and the sides. Set aside a few slices of cake.

3. Pour the syrup over the slices of fruit cake, to soak.

4. Add scoops of ice cream to the bowl and arrange over the soaked cake, to fill to the top.

5. Using the back of a spoon, press and flatten.

6. Arrange the set-aside slices of cake on the top to completely cover the surface.

7. Fold the overhanging plastic wrap over the sides and fold it neatly over the cake, covering the entire bowl. Arrange a dinner plate over the top and gently press to even out the surface.

8. Transfer to the freezer for 2-4 hours.

9. In a double boiler, melt the chocolate.

10. Remove the ice cream from the freezer.

11. Take the wrap off the bowl and invert the frozen ice cream onto a plate.

12. Pour the melted chocolate over the fruitcake and allow it to drip all over the ball.

13. Serve.

Caramel Banana Cake Bars

Princes Harry and William love banana cake, and in fact, there were rumors that Harry and Meghan were going to choose a banana flavor cake for their wedding - they didn't, but we are sure your friends and family will go bananas for this recipe!

Servings: 24 bars

Total Time: 1hour 20mins

Ingredients:

- 2 tsp butter (to grease)

Cake:

- ½ cup butter
- ¾ cup light brown sugar
- 2 medium eggs
- 1 cup bananas (mashed)
- 1½ cups self rising flour
- 1 tsp bicarb of soda
- ¾ cup sour cream
- 1 tbsp whole milk
- 1 tsp vanilla essence

Frosting:

- ¾ cup unsalted butter
- 1 cup light brown sugar
- ¼ cup sour cream
- 3 cups confectioner's sugar
- 1 tsp vanilla essence

Directions:

1. Preheat the main oven to 350 degrees F. Lightly grease a baking pan with 2 teaspoons of butter.

2. First, prepare the cake by creaming the butter along with the sugar and until fluffy.

3. Add the eggs and mashed bananas and beat to combine. Stir in the flour along with the bicarb of soda, sour cream, milk and vanilla essence until the batter is lump-free and smooth.

4. Pour the mixture into the baking pan and bake on the middle shelf of the preheated oven for 40 minutes, or until the cake is springy to the touch.

5. Set the cake to one side before frosting.

6. Next, make the frosting. In a pan, melt the butter along with the sugar.

7. Stir for a couple of minutes, without boiling.

8. Pour in the sour cream and bring to a boil.

9. Remove the pan from the heat and stir in the confectioner's sugar followed by the vanilla essence.

10. Allow the frosting to cool and thicken a little before frosting.

11. Cut into bars and enjoy.

Chocolate Fridge Cake

Enjoy Prince William and Catherine Middleton's favorite dessert, and chosen groom's cake, which is surprisingly simple to whip up!

Servings: 12-14

Total Time: 8hours 15mins

Ingredients:

- 2 meringue nests (broken)
- 3½ ounces pecans (chopped)
- 7 ounces plain digestive biscuits
- 10 glace cherries (chopped)
- 3¾ ounces pistachios (chopped)
- 7 ounces 70% cocoa dark chocolate (chopped)
- 1 tbsp golden syrup/treacle
- 5¼ ounces unsalted butter (chopped)

Directions:

1. Line a loaf tin with plastic kitchen wrap, leaving plenty of overhang.

2. Add the meringue, pecans, biscuits, cherries, and pistachios to a bowl. Toss to combine.

3. Melt the dark chocolate in a double boiler, add the treacle and chopped butter stirring until melted and incorporated.

4. Take off the heat and pour over the meringue/pecan mixture until combined.

5. Spoon into the loaf tin and chill overnight.

6. When ready to serve, thickly slice.

Danish Wedding Cookies

The tradition of giving newlywed couples cookies to celebrate their marriage dates back centuries. They are thought to bring good luck, with the nuts representing 'bumps in the road' and the powdered sugar symbolizing the 'sweetness' that comes from a happy marriage.

Servings: 24

Total Time: 30mins

Ingredients:

- Butter (for greasing)
- ¼ tsp cinnamon
- 1¼ cups all-purpose flour
- ¾ cup pecans (chopped)
- ½ cup salted butter (at room temperature)
- ½ tsp vanilla essence
- ½ cup confectioner's sugar
- 1½ cups confectioner's sugar (for serving)

Directions:

1. Preheat the main oven to 400 degrees F and lightly grease a baking sheet.

2. Add the cinnamon and flour to a bowl and stir to combine.

3. In a second bowl, beat together the pecans, butter, vanilla essence, and ½ cup of confectioner's sugar. Mix in the flour/cinnamon until combined but stiff.

4. Roll the mixture into small balls and arrange on the baking sheet.

5. Place in the oven and bake for just over 10 minutes.

6. Add the 1½ cups confectioner's sugar to a bowl.

7. While the cookies are still warm, roll them in the sugar. Allow to completely cool before enjoying.

Eton Mess Raspberry Royale

A quintessentially British dessert ideal for summer and most definitely fit for a royal!

Servings: 4

Total Time: 35mins

Ingredients:

- 2 cups fresh raspberries
- 2 ounces cognac
- 2 ounces superfine sugar
- 2-3 drops vanilla essence
- 3 ounces powdered sugar
- 18 ounces heavy whipping cream
- 8 individual-size meringue nests (broken into pieces)

Directions:

1. Set aside a small handful of raspberries for topping.

2. Add the remaining raspberries to a bowl with the cognac and superfine sugar, crush to combine then set aside for half an hour.

3. Whip up the vanilla essence, powdered sugar, and cream until soft but firm.

4. Add the mashed raspberry mixture to the cream and fold the two together, do not fully combine, the mixture should look marbled.

5. Fold in the broken meringue. Spoon into dishes and garnish with a few whole raspberries.

Jelly-Filled Heart Donuts

A famous USA fast food restaurant chain has created the Royal Love doughnut which will only be available for 6 days in mid-May. Just in case you miss out, here, is our sweet heart-shaped donut recipe.

Servings: 3

Total Time: 30mins

Ingredients:

Donuts:

- ¾ cup whole wheat flour
- ½ cup pumpkin puree
- 1 tsp baking powder
- 1 tbsp olive oil
- 1 tsp liquid sweetener
- 1 tbsp baking cocoa
- 1 tsp apple cider vinegar

Filling:

- ¼ cup raspberries
- 2 tbsp vanilla protein powder
- Milk (as needed)
- Glaze:
- Vanilla protein powder (as needed)
- Water (as needed)
- Rainbow sprinkles (optional)

Directions:

1. Combine the flour with the pumpkin puree, baking powder, olive oil, sweetener, baking cocoa and cider vinegar until a dough begins to forms. Using clean hands, fully combine.

2. Divide the dough into 3 evenly-sized portions and make into heart shapes.

3. Place the hearts on a microwave-safe plate and microwave for 3 minutes. Set to one side to cool down.

4. Using a drinking straw, press into the side of each of the donuts and scoop out some of the dough to make room for the jelly fillings.

5. In a microwave-safe bowl, microwave the berries until softened.

6. Combine with the protein powder along with sufficient milk to make the mixture creamy and smooth.

7. Pipe the jam filling into each of the 3 donuts.

8. To make the glaze mix a small amount of protein powder with a drop of water.

9. Dip the tops of the doughnuts into the glaze.

10. Decorate with sprinkles and enjoy.

Lavender Shortbread

Not only does the Duchess of Cornwall adore lavender shortbread, but she shared her love of these tasty morsels as a way to help combat the Duchess of Cambridge (Kate Middleton's) morning sickness. They are the perfect nibble for a bridal or baby shower.

Servings: 20

Total Time: 45mins

Ingredients:

- 12¼ ounces butter (room temperature)
- 7 ounces fine demerara sugar
- 1 pound plain flour
- 2-3 tbsp culinary, edible lavender (to taste)

Directions:

1. Preheat the main oven to 320 degrees F.

2. In a bowl, cream the butter with the sugar until combined.

3. Add 14 ounces of the flour along with 2-3 tbsp of culinary lavender and mix thoroughly.

4. A little at a time add more flour until it has all been used and a soft dough forms.

5. Scatter the remaining flour over a clean worktop; this will prevent the dough from sticking.

6. Roll the dough out to approximately ⅓" thickness. Cut into strips of around 2¾ x¾".

7. Prick each strip with a metal fork and arrange, not touching, on a baking tray, lightly greased with butter.

8. Bake in the preheated oven for between 15-20 minutes until golden.

9. Transfer the shortbread to a wire baking rack and serve.

Lemon and Elderflower Drizzle Cake

Prince Harry and Megan Markle's delicious spring-inspired elderflower and lemon wedding cake was crafted by master baker Clair Ptak. Don't worry though; you don't need to be a cake expert to enjoy these delicious fresh flavors thanks to our simple drizzle cake recipe.

Servings: 12

Total Time: 1hour 30mins

Ingredients:

- Butter (for greasing)
- 8 ounces superfine sugar
- 8 ounces salted butter (at room temperature)
- Juice and zest of 1 medium lemon
- 4 eggs
- 8 ounces self-raising flour
- 2 tbsp hot water
- 4 ounces elderflower liqueur*
- 2 tbsp white sugar

Directions:

1. Preheat the main oven to 360 degrees F. Grease an 8" springform cake tin with butter and line with parchment.

2. Beat together the superfine sugar, butter, and lemon zest using an electric whisk.

3. With the whisk running, crack in the eggs and continue to mix until incorporated. When cracking in the final egg, sprinkle in 2 tbsp of the flour to help prevent splitting.

4. Sift the remaining flour into the batter, pour in the hot water and use a metal spoon to fold the mixture until just combined.

5. Pour the batter into the cake tin and place in the oven. Bake for just over 45 minutes until golden. Take out of the oven and allow to cool a little.

6. In the meantime, stir together the lemon juice and elderflower liqueur.

7. Poke holes in the warm cake using a skewer and evenly pour over the liqueur mixture. Quickly sprinkle the cake with the white sugar. Allow the cake to completely cool before lifting out of the cake tin.

*For a child-friendly alternative, use elderflower cordial.

Mexican Wedding Biscuits

The exact origin of these buttery, nutty biscuit bites is unknown. However, their popularity is indisputable. They make a wonderful wedding favor or dessert buffet addition.

Servings: 18

Total Time: 3hours 35mins

Ingredients:

- ½ cup granulated sugar
- 1 cup salted butter
- 2 tsp water
- 2 tsp vanilla essence
- 1 cup almonds (chopped)
- 2 cups all-purpose flour
- ½ cup powdered sugar

Directions:

1. Beat together the sugar and butter, stir in the water and vanilla essence.

2. Finally, stir in the chopped almonds and flour. Cover with plastic wrap and chill for a few hours.

3. Preheat the main oven to 325 degrees F.

4. Roll the dough into smooth balls; you should have approximately 18 dough balls.

5. Arrange the balls on cookie sheets and place in the oven. Bake for 15-17 minutes until lightly golden.

6. Add the powdered sugar to a bowl.

7. While the cookies are still warm, roll in the sugar to coat. Allow to completely cool before serving.

Peppermint Ice Cream

Although married in the winter of 1973, Princess Anne and Captain Mark Phillips opted for a frozen dessert of peppermint ice cream.

Servings: 7 cups

Total Time: 8hours 40mins

Ingredients:

- 3 cups heavy cream
- 2 cups whole milk
- 1 cup granulated sugar (divided)
- Pinch kosher salt
- 10 medium egg yolks
- ¼ tsp peppermint oil

Directions:

1. In a large pan, combine the heavy cream with the milk along with ½ of the sugar and a pinch of salt. Heat to a gentle simmer over moderately high heat, while occasionally stirring. Remove the pan from the heat.

2. Add the egg yolks along with the remaining sugar in a large bowl and on moderate speed, mix for a couple of minutes until pale yellow and thick.

3. In a steady, slow stream, add 1 cup of the warmed cream mixture to the egg mixture. When incorporated, pour the yolk mixture into the pan with the remaining cream mixture.

4. Cook while continually stirring over moderately low heat, until the mixture is sufficiently thick enough to easily coat the back of a spoon.

5. Strain the mixture through a fine mesh strainer placed over a bowl.

6. Add the peppermint oil and stir.

7. Cover with kitchen wrap, ensuring that the wrap is touching the surface of the custard. Transfer to the fridge to chill.

8. Pour the chilled mixture into an ice cream maker and churn according to the manufacturer instructions. This should take around 20 minutes.

9. Transfer the peppermint ice cream to the freezer to completely harden, for 4-8 hours.

Princess Diana's Boozy Bread and Butter Pudding

This year, why not honor the Royal Wedding by baking up a batch of the groom's mother's (Princess Diana) favorite dessert of caramelized bread and butter pudding with toasted almonds?

Servings: 8

Total Time: 9hours 10mins

Ingredients:

- 4 tbsp almond liqueur
- 3 ounces sultanas
- Nonstick spray
- 4 ounces unsalted butter (at room temperature)
- 12 slices white bread (crusts removed)
- 5 ounces superfine sugar
- Yolks of 9 large eggs
- 12 ounces heavy cream
- 5 ounces whole milk
- 1 vanilla pod (split)
- Hot water
- 3 ounces toasted flaked almonds
- 1 tsp confectioner's sugar

Directions:

1. Add the liqueur and sultanas to a bowl, cover and set aside overnight.

2. The following day, preheat the main oven to 350 degrees F and spritz a baking dish with nonstick spray.

3. Butter the bread slices. Take 3 of the slices and cut into ½" cubes, slice the remaining bread into triangles and set both to one side for a moment.

4. Whisk together the superfine sugar and yolks. Set to one side.

5. In a saucepan over moderate heat, add the cream, milk, and vanilla stirring to combine. When the mixture comes to a simmer, take off the heat and pour over the egg yolk/sugar mixture whisking well to combine and form a smooth custard.

6. Remove the vanilla pod halves scraping the seeds from them into the custard before discarding.

7. Begin to assemble the pudding. Arrange the bread cubes in an even layer in the base of the dish. Scatter with the soaked sultanas and liqueur.

8. Arrange the bread triangles on top in overlapped rows.

9. Pour the custard mixture slowly and evenly over the bread and set aside for half an hour.

10. In the meantime, find a roasting tin larger than your baking dish and place the dish inside.

11. After the half an hour soaking time has elapsed, pour hot water into the roasting tin until it reaches ¾ of the way up the side of the baking dish. Take care not to splash any water into the pudding.

12. Pop in the oven and bake for half an hour until the custard is firm and set. Allow to cool a little.

13. Before serving, scatter the warm pudding with the flaked almonds and sprinkle with confectioner's sugar.

Queen of Puddings

This recipe goes all the way back to the 17th century, and it truly is, a pudding fit for a queen.

Portions: 6

Total Time: 1hour 40mins

Ingredients:

- Butter (to grease)
- 4 cups whole milk
- 4 tbsp unsalted butter
- 1 cup granulated sugar (divided)
- 1½ tsp fresh lemon zest (grated)
- ¾ tsp salt
- 1 pound white sandwich bread (crusts removed, cut into cubes)
- 4 medium egg yolks
- ½ cup blackcurrant jam
- 5 medium egg whites

Directions:

1. Preheat the main oven to 355 degrees F.

2. Using butter, lightly grease 6 gratin dishes and put to one side.

3. In a pan bring the milk to simmer along with the butter, half of the sugar, zest, and salt. Stir well, add the cubes of bread and remove from the heat. Set to one side for 30 minutes, returning every 5-7 minutes to stir.

4. Add the egg yolks and stir to combine.

5. Evenly divide the custard into the 6 gratin dishes.

6. Bake in the oven for 13-15 minutes, until just set. Set to one side to cool.

7. Turn the oven temperature down to 325 degrees F.

8. In a pan, add the jam and heat for between 3-5 minutes until thinned.

9. Spread the jam evenly over each of the cooled puddings.

10. Bring a pan of water to a simmer. Set a heatproof bowl on the top of the pan.

11. Add the egg whites along with the remaining sugar into the bowl and whisk for a couple of minutes.

12. Remove from the heat and continue whisking until medium peaks begin to form

13. Spoon the meringue evenly onto the 6 puddings allowing a half inch border free of meringue.

14. Place the puddings in the oven and bake for 10-12 minutes.

15. Serve at once and enjoy.

Rhubarb Creme Brulee

You will love this sharp crème brulee which is very much like the delicious dessert of Rhubard Crème Brulee Tartlets enjoyed by Prince William and Kate Middleton at their wedding.

Servings: 4

Total Time: 8hours 45mins

Ingredients:

- 14 ounces rhubarb, trimmed and cut into 1cm pieces
- 9 tbsp golden caster sugar
- 4 medium egg yolks
- 15¼ ounces double cream
- 1 vanilla pod (seeds scraped, reserved)

Directions:

1. Preheat the main oven to 400 degrees F.

2. Add the rhubarb to a roasting tin along with 3 tbsp of sugar, tossing to coat.

3. Roast in the oven until the rhubarb is softened.

4. Divided the rhubarb between 4 (6 ¾ ounce) flameproof ramekins. Transfer to the fridge to chill.

5. Add 4 tbsp of sugar along with the egg yolks to a large bowl, whisking until pale.

6. Add the double cream and vanilla pod seeds to a heavy saucepan and over moderate heat, warm until the cream bubbles around the edges.

7. A little at a time pour the now warmed cream into the bowl containing the egg yolks and whisk until silky smooth.

8. Return the mixture to the pan and gently, over low heat, stir for 20 minutes, until the custard easily coats the back of a spoon.

9. Pour the custard into a pitcher or jug and pour over the individual ramekins.

10. Transfer to the fridge overnight.

11. Scatter the remaining sugar over the top of the custards and with a crème brulee blow torch evenly brown the sugar.

12. Serve when the sugar is hard, 2-3 minutes.

13. Serve.

Spanish Wedding Cake

Spanish wedding cake is an all-together simpler affair than a royal iced and decorated British wedding cake, making it an ideal choice for more relaxed and intimate wedding celebrations.

Servings: 12-14

Total Time: 1hour 30mins

Ingredients:

- Butter (for greasing)
- 2 cups granulated sugar
- 2 cups plain flour
- 2 tsp bicarb of soda
- 2 medium eggs (well beaten)
- 1 (20 ounce) can crushed pineapple and juice

Frosting:

- 8 ounces full-fat cream cheese
- ½ cup salted butter
- 3½ cups confectioner's sugar

Directions:

1. Preheat the main oven to 350 degrees F and lightly grease a 13x9" cake tin.

2. Beat together the sugar, flour, bicarb of soda, eggs, and pineapple until combined. Transfer the batter to the cake tin.

3. Place in the oven and bake for just over half an hour until golden and set. Allow to completely cool.

4. Next, make the frosting, whisk together the cream cheese, butter, and sugar until thick and fluffy. Roughly spread the frosting onto the cooled cake, it needs to be even but not too neat.

5. Slice into squares and serve.

About the Author

Martha is a chef and a cookbook author. She has had a love of all things culinary since she was old enough to help in the kitchen, and hasn't wanted to leave the kitchen since. She was born and raised in Illinois, and grew up on a farm, where she acquired her love for fresh, delicious foods. She learned many of her culinary abilities from her mother; most importantly, the need to cook with fresh, homegrown ingredients if at all possible, and how to create an amazing recipe that everyone wants. This gave her the perfect way to share her skill with the world; writing cookbooks to spread the message that fresh, healthy food really can, and does, taste delicious. Now that she is a mother, it is more important than ever to make sure that healthy food is available to the next generation. She hopes to become a household name in cookbooks for her delicious recipes, and healthy outlook.

Martha is now living in California with her high school sweetheart, and now husband, John, as well as their infant daughter Isabel, and two dogs; Daisy and Sandy. She is a stay at home mom, who is very much looking forward to expanding their family in the next few years to give their daughter some siblings. She enjoys cooking with, and for, her family and friends, and is waiting impatiently for the day she can start cooking with her daughter.

Author's Afterthoughts

Thanks ever so much to each of my cherished readers for investing the time to read this book!

I know you could have picked from many other books but you chose this one. So a big thanks for downloading this book and reading all the way to the end.

If you enjoyed this book or received value from it, I'd like to ask you for a favor. Please take a few minutes to post an honest and heartfelt review on Amazon.com. Your support does make a difference and helps to benefit other people.

Thanks!

Martha Stephenson.